Victorian Electroplate

Shirley Bury

The Beginnings   3

Struggle and Success   12

Consolidation and Decline   39

Marks   62

COUNTRY LIFE COLLECTORS' GUIDES

Electroplated egg frame.
Height 10 in. Unmarked,
except for one spoon; by
Henry Wilkinson,
Sheffield. The other
(silver) spoons are
replacements. About
1870. Private collection.

The Beginnings

Numbers in the margin refer to the page where an illustration may be found

On 25th March 1840 George Richards Elkington (1800–1865) and his cousin Henry Elkington (about 1810–1852), both Birmingham manufacturers, took out a patent for electroplating and electrogilding (no. 8447), thus formally launching the commercial development of a process which was to kill off Sheffield plate in the course of the next few decades. The two Elkingtons were not the inventors of electroplating, nor were they the first to patent the use of an electric current to coat one metal with another. Three weeks earlier than they, a Birmingham merchant named Joseph Shore applied for Letters Patent for electroplating with copper and nickel; the Elkingtons' advantage was that their process used gold and silver instead. Compared with some of the great names engaged in research into electrical phenomena in the 18th and early 19th century, none of the three Birmingham men ranks as an original thinker. In industrial technology, however, the Elkingtons had a far-reaching effect, for they changed the face of the silver and plating trades all over the world.

Centuries earlier, before the laws governing electrical action had been understood and formulated, its accidental effects were regarded as evidence of magic. This attitude persisted for a long time. In his *Travels* of 1685, Dr Edward Browne described a Hungarian mine which had 'two springs of vitriolat water which turn iron into copper'. This was not alchemy: the mine probably contained copper sulphate in solution which resulted in the iron receiving a coating of copper.

Posthumous portrait by Samuel West of G.R. Elkington, painted just after his death in 1865. Presented by Elkington & Company to the City Museum and Art Gallery, Birmingham.

The aura of magic surrounding the subject was gradually to be dissipated by scientific research. For a while, Birmingham provided the setting for one of the 18th-century investigators who contributed to the total sum of knowledge on the subject. He was Joseph Priestley, who belonged to the Lunar Society, a scientific discussion group founded in about 1766, which received its name because its meetings were held monthly on the Monday nearest to the full moon. A great manufacturer, Matthew Boulton, was a joint founder of the society, proof of his appreciation of the benefits afforded to industry by science; and another, Josiah Wedgwood, was amongst the members.

The work of 18th-century researchers was to some extent in-

Plating dynamo built by Thomas Prime & Son, Northwood Street, Birmingham, in 1844. Science Museum, Birmingham.

hibited by the sporadic action of the frictional electric machines then in use. The drawback was removed when Alessandro Volta, Professor of Physics at the University of Pavia, invented the electric pile in about 1800. Volta's own work was in part a development of the studies of another Italian, Luigi Galvani, who had induced muscular contractions in frogs by means of electricity. Galvani was so celebrated that for much of the 19th century the term galvanism was synonymous with electricity, while Volta in turn lent his name to the pile he invented, which was known as the voltaic cell. Volta's battery became the source of an electric current which could be used to deposit metals from solutions.

Using the cell, William Cruickshank observed its effects on silver and copper in 1804, and a year later Luigi Vincenzo Brugnatelli, born in Pavia where Volta worked, wrote to tell a colleague that he 'had gilt in a complete manner two large silver medals, by bringing them into communication by means of a steel wire with the negative pole of a voltaic pile, newly made and well saturated'. As electrogilding was an actuality in 1805, it is extraordinary that thirty-five years were allowed to elapse before the process was patented. The difficulty was that it was still in the experimental stage; and as investigation progressed, it was discovered that the voltaic pile itself had serious limitations, growing steadily weaker in action and finally fading out altogether.

Despite these and other problems, great advances were made in research, and the more progressively minded members of the silver trade began to contemplate the prospect of turning electrometallurgy to their own advantage. While men like Sir Humphry Davy studied electrolytic phenomena and Michael Faraday, his former pupil, discovered electromagnetism, the trade had already begun to conduct its own experiments. An obvious field was electrogilding. The traditional technique of mercury-gilding silver produced a beautiful and lasting effect, but it killed off the craftsmen who practised it. Mercury piosoning ensured that few of them lived until middle age.

Rundell, Bridge & Rundell, Royal Goldsmiths for the first four decades of the 19th century, seem to have made a trial run of 7 electrogilding in 1814, using it to decorate a silver **goblet** which survives in the royal collections. The piece was made by Paul Storr, the firm's principal silversmith, from a design by John Flaxman. An inventory of the royal plate compiled by Rundell's for William IV in 1832 described it as 'A very small Galvanic Goblet, with basso relievo of the Hours'. Unhappily, no records survive to show whether the firm produced other examples of electrogilding. Rundell's went into dissolution in 1842 and all their ledgers and correspondence were destroyed.

Public interest in electro-metallurgy was always very lively. The dichotomy between the arts and the sciences which characterises our own day did not then exist to such an acute degree, and many people whom we should now associate exclusively with the arts were fascinated by the subject. While at Marischal College, Aberdeen, William Dyce, afterwards to become celebrated as a painter who anticipated many of the ideas of the

'Galvanic Goblet'. Height 5 in. London hallmark for 1814; maker's mark of Paul Storr. Royal collections.

Pre-Raphaelite Brotherhood, won the Blackwell Prize of 1830 with an essay on electromagnetism. Nearly twenty years later, Mary Ann Evans, not yet metamorphosed into the novelist George Eliot, spent the winter at Geneva and attended the open lectures for ladies given by Professor A.A. de la Rive, an authority on electrogilding.

Electrogilding and electroplating are the same process in essence, the difference lying in the metal deposited. Both represent the final skin given to otherwise finished and decorated base metal articles. A related process developed in the 1830s resulted in the whole object being grown, as it were, in the plating vat. It was hailed as the electrical equivalent of casting and was known as electrotyping or, inspired by continental usage, galvanoplastik.

Many commentators claimed that the process originated in the

The National Medallion. Diameter 5.7 in. Original wax sketch model (*left*) and two trial electrotypes. The design by Antoine Vechte (1799–1868). Victoria and Albert Museum, London.

, Thomas Spencer, a Liverpool framemaker, and a London craftsman, C.J. Jordan, all independently succeeded in making copper replicas of medals and similar small objects on the same principle. As the technique was developed, it was usually found necessary to make a mould from the object to be reproduced. This provided a negative from which a positive metal cast was made. Finally, a negative metal mould was produced from the cast, into which the copper was deposited. This procedure was

years to [...]

Von Jacobi, Spe[...] England within a few months of each other [...] had gone into print elsewhere earlier, but the other two men were unaware of his work. It was later claimed that John Stephen Woolrich of Birmingham, an enemy of the Elkingtons of whom we shall hear more presently, made similar experiments, but if so, he did not publish them. Meanwhile, the Elkington cousins had already embarked on the research which led to their patent of 1840. Strictly speaking, electrotyping was excluded from this patent, except in so far as their plating solutions were concerned, but they were quick to establish their claim to the technique by patenting a series of improvements evolved by their principal metallurgist, Alexander Parkes, which were especially useful when articles of more complicated form than medals were reproduced. Jordan withdrew from the field; von Jacobi was too far away to present an immediate threat; and the cousins prudently engaged Spencer as an aide, employing him to sell licences to operate their patented processes to silversmiths in Liverpool and elsewhere.

The Elkingtons had already decided upon their policy. They would recruit the best chemists they could find and take out as many patents as possible in England and abroad. They would buy up rival patents, however expensive, if it was felt that these constituted a real threat, and they would do their best to neutralise the inventors by employing them, at least on a temporary basis. They were determined to create the right conditions in the trade to sweep the board with their patent, for they believed that unlike all their competitors, scientific and commercial, they possessed the secret not only of plating and gilding on a large scale, but of making the coatings of precious metal adhere permanently.

G.R. Elkington's signature on the final agreement between him, Henry Elkington and John Wright relating to the 1840 patent. The agreement is dated 4th January 1842.

A letter dated 10th March 1840 from Benjamin Smith to G.R. Elkington: 'Dear Sir, I am very anxious to know how your arrangements for silvering proceed – will you be so good as to inform me of this by return. I am Your very obedient Servant Benjamin Smith'.

Struggle and
Success

G. R. and Henry Elkington went into partnership together some time after 1829 and probably before 1836. Until 1829 G. R. Elkington has been associated with his uncle George Richards, to whom he had earlier been apprenticed. The Richards-Elkington business had made and sold spectacles and 'gilt toys' (not playthings, but small articles like snuffboxes and personal adornments of a type traditionally manufactured in Birmingham). The cousins continued this trade, with individual variations, and they were naturally interested in discovering new methods of gilding base metal.

Their researches led to three patents. The first (no. 7134) was granted on 24th June 1836 to G. R. Elkington; the second (no. 7304) on 17th February 1837 to Henry; and the third (no. 7496) on 4th December 1837 to Henry again. In order to exploit his patent, G. R. Elkington formed a subsidiary partnership in 1837 with two buttonmaking firms in Birmingham. One of these concerns was Hardman & Iliffe's; and it is amusing to reflect that their interest in modern technology helped to underpin the activities of the first of the so-called 'Medieval Metalworkers' of the Victorian age, John Hardman & Company. The younger Hardman had become, with his father, a co-partner of Elkington when he met the architect Augustus Welby Northmore Pugin. Inspired by Pugin, who became his designer, Hardman began in 1838 to combine his buttonmaking with the production of church furnishings in the Gothic manner.

Pugin repeatedly stressed his contempt for everything to do with the Industrial Revolution in his books and lectures. He always claimed in public that he and Hardman had dedicated themselves to the revival of both medieval design and craftsmanship. He never openly admitted to the connection with Elkington's, but the surviving records of John Hardman & Company show that modern technology went hand-in-hand with the hand-raising, enamelling and other traditional techniques practised by the firm. They made some electrotypes; they frequently produced communion vessels of silver-plated nickel alloy, a material unknown in the Middle Ages, and they seem to have used the electrogilding process to decorate much of their work, even their 13 elaborately worked **chalices**. Pugin himself was perfectly aware

Pair of gilt copper chalices, enamelled and set with gems. Height $9\frac{1}{4}$ in. Made by John Hardman & Company from a design by A. W. N. Pugin. 1850. Church of St Barnabas, Pimlico, London.

of all these departures from the theoretical ideal of craftsmanship, as he often ordered plated articles for his own domestic use.

While a great many of the original documents relating to the Elkingtons' activities have also been preserved, there are no contemporary notes on the experiments which led up to the gilding patents, so that we have no means of knowing how closely they were both concerned in the work. They employed assistants even at that time. The most important, Alexander Parkes, was certainly working for the Elkingtons by the late 1830s; he earned more than £200 for his help in preparing the specification of the 1840 patent. It would be surprising, even so, if the cousins had not played an active part in the experiments. They had both

The Elkington factory and showrooms in Newhall Street, Birmingham; now demolished. Lithograph from *Cornish's Guide to Birmingham and its Manufactories*, 1855.

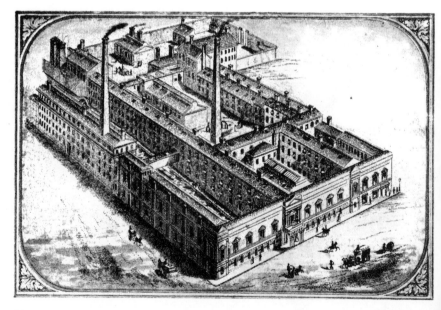

served an apprenticeship in the metal trades of Birmingham where, as in Sheffield, there was a strong economic incentive to technical innovation.

The gilding patents did not specify electrical action, but their research clearly led the Elkingtons to consider it as a possibility. On 24th July 1838, G. R. Elkington and Oglethorpe Wakelin Barratt took out a patent (no. 7742) for coating metals with zinc which hints at the use of an electrical circuit. G. R. Elkington must have been convinced by this time that he was on the right track, for he was building a large and impressive **factory** in Newhall Street, Birmingham, with the assistance of one of the Hardmans. After the second World War, the factory became for a time the home of the Birmingham Science Museum, but it has since been demolished.

Barratt was one of Elkington's less willing collaborators, whose services had to be purchased to prevent him from becoming a potential rival. Two subsequent patents applied for in Barratt's name were in reality the property of G. R. and Henry Elkington, much of the work on them having been done at their expense. Barratt also helped with the 1840 patent, but he cannot have contributed much to the final specification for, as we shall see, the decisive element came from outside.

All the evidence goes to show that serious research on the project was well under way in 1839. In December of that year G. R. Elkington alluded to the slow progress being made in a letter to the London silversmith **Benjamin Smith**, son of the Benjamin who had worked for Rundell, Bridge & Rundell, the Royal Gold-smiths, in the early years of the century. Smith had sent some base metal articles to be silvered by the Elkington firm, but the 'improvements' they were struggling to effect in Birmingham resulted in delays. Despite the inconvenience to him, Smith saw great possibilities in the process, and after the patent was taken out he entered into a series of agreements with the Birmingham firm which resulted in his setting up electroplating workshops in Moorgate, City of London, together with retail premises in Regent Street, both in the name of Elkington & Company.

The association, begun so cordially, ended in tragedy for Smith.

His own silversmithing concern at Duke Street, Lincolns Inn Fields, London, occupied much of his time, and he was discouraged in his management of the plating workshops by the hostility he met with from some sections of the trade. G. R. Elkington severed the connection towards the end of 1849, taking over the London premises himself and driving the unfortunate Smith into bankruptcy the following year. Smith was relieved from experiencing the full ignominy of the proceedings by his own death, which occurred in May 1850 after an illness of some seven months' duration.

Earlier, when relations between them were still harmonious, Smith had supplied the Elkingtons with designs for their electroplated wares: the **'crown imperial' salad stand** almost certainly came from his artists, and probably also the **fruit dish** in the form of a vine-leaf. With its flowers gilt, the salad stand cost £18 13s.; plain electroplate was a guinea less. The fruit dish cost £3 5s. gilt and £2 plain. They were neither exactly cheap, although they were undeniably less expensive than silver. The Elkingtons were having to recoup their massive investment in research. The designs, however, probably cost them little or nothing, as the obligation to provide them was laid upon Smith by the terms of his agreements.

Benjamin had always claimed in his replies to G. R. Elkington's complaints about poor business in London that it was difficult to get large orders from manufacturers and retailers in the city. He probably met with a cautious response from the people he approached, but equally Elkington's suspicions that Smith was not trying as hard as he should have done may well have been justified. Temperamentally, it seems, Smith was unsuited to the task, for there is evidence from other sources that resistance to the new process had begun to weaken by 1843. At least, it is clear that the Sheffield plate trade was already beginning to suffer from the introduction of electroplating. The platers' natural reaction was to vilify the Elkingtons, and they found several scientists sufficiently resentful of the 1840 patent, which they saw as impinging on their own research, to join in the hue and cry. It was said, loudly and often, that the Elkingtons had no right to the patent.

The cousins were even accused of having conducted no experiments at all, which was not the case.

Nevertheless, there was some basis for the accusations. The key electrolyte in the patent specification contained potassium cyanide, and it was this that ensured a firmer plating than had previously been achieved, except erratically and almost by chance. The electrolyte was the invention of John Wright, a surgeon working in Birmingham, who was led to experiment after reading a passage in Scheele's *Chemical Essays*, in which reference was made to the solubility of the cyanides of gold and silver in potassium cyanide.

Electroplated salad stand inspired by the crown imperial lily, shown by Elkington, Mason & Company at the Birmingham Exhibition of 1849 and the Great Exhibition of 1851. Lithograph from an Elkington Catalogue of 1852.

Electroplated fruit dish in the form of a vine-leaf. Benjamin Smith showed a variant of this design at the Manchester Exhibition of 1845–1846. Lithograph from an Elkington Catalogue of 1852.

Electroplated teapot by Elkington, Mason & Company, and the marks appearing on its base. The 'O' is the firm's date letter for 1853 (see page 62). Height $7\frac{1}{8}$ in. Assay Office Collection, Birmingham.

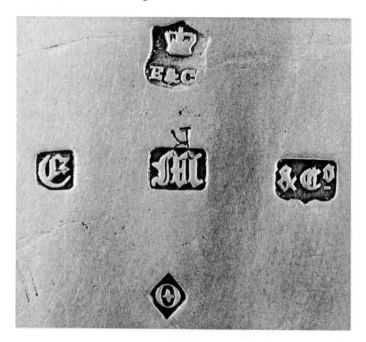

According to a confidential statement made by G. R. Elkington to his legal advisers a few years later, his attention was drawn to Wright's discovery only a few weeks before the specification had to be enrolled on 25th October, the end of the six months' grace allowed after the patent was applied for. On the advice of his friend Charles Askin, a brilliant amateur chemist who was the first to refine nickel by chemical means, Wright refused to divulge the details of his research to Elkington until a binding agreement was reached between them. When this was negotiated, there were only a few days to go, and in Elkington's words, he and his colleagues then found Wright's process to be 'the same in principle as we were about to specify and we decided to embrace the variation, which consisted of a different solution, in our specification'. The Elkingtons had been working on a solution of ammonia. Their purchase from Wright cost them more than the money they paid him, for the sense of unease engendered by their use of his discovery probably accounts for the wholesale manner in which they subsequently bought up rival patents.

In order to finance their activities on such an amitious scale, the Elkingtons took on a third partner in 1842. He was Josiah Mason, a wealthy pen manufacturer with whom G. R. Elkington had already had financial dealings. The firm now became known as Elkington, Mason & Company, although they did not entirely abandon the old style of Elkington & Company. From this time, their electroplate was **marked** with 'E & Co.' in a shield, and 'E M & Co.' in three separate shields, together with their own private date letter sequence which indicates the year of manufacture (see page 62). Henry Elkington's retirement and death in 1852 did not affect these marks; Mason left the firm in about 1859, although the mark incorporating his initial was not finally dropped until 1864. It need scarcely be remarked that these stamps and their placing were inspired by the form of hallmarks: this was an old practice instituted by the Sheffield platers, and one on which the Assay Offices kept a watchful eye to see that the marks were not too like those legally denoting silver.

One of the acquisitions made by Elkington, Mason & Company in accordance with the purchasing policy was Joseph Shore's

patent of 3rd March 1840 (see page 3). Shore admitted that the experiments made prior to the patent were conducted with the aid of J. S. Woolrich, who was always a thorn in the Elkingtons' flesh. On 1st August 1842 Woolrich himself obtained Letters Patent (no. 9431) for the first plating dynamo, which owed its existence to Faraday's work on magneto-electric currents in the
5 early 1830s. The **dynamo** illustrated was built by Thomas Prime of Birmingham to Woolrich's specifications in 1844 and remained in use until 1877. Faraday and his wife are said to have inspected it on a visit to Prime's electroplating workshops in the 1840s.

Henry Elkington acquired the patent rights of the dynamo on

behalf of his firm in May 1846, after licences to use the invention had already been granted to Prime and two Sheffield manufacturers, William Carr Hutton and William Briggs (the latter founded the firm later to be known as Roberts & Belk). The Elkington firm had a huge **magneto machine** made to incorporate subsequent modifications which deposited fifty ounces of silver an hour.

Happily for the Elkingtons, not all inventors were as uncooperative as Woolrich: they were eventually forced to purchase the patent rights of his machine from a third party to whom he had sold it earlier. On the other hand, several scientists such as

Elkington's improved plating dynamo in operation at Newhall Street, Birmingham, serving the plating vats on the right. Woodcut from Cassell's *Illustrated Exhibitor*, I, 1852.

Dr H. B. Leeson showed themselves very willing to help. On 1st June 1842 Leeson patented on the firm's behalf a series of 'improvements' which included more than four hundred salts and compounds not before used in electrolytic solutions (no. 9374). Amongst the contributions made by Elkington's own permanent staff in the 1840s, the patent issued to William Millward and Morris Lyons on 23rd March 1847 (no. 11,632) is worthy of mention. Millward was actually the person who hit on the invention, a formula for depositing silver so that it needed comparatively little subsequent burnishing. The method was known as 'bright plating'. It is said that Lyons became co-patentee solely because he overheard Millward discussing his invention and threatened to disclose the secret unless he was bought off.

Some of the early patents obtained by the Elkingtons' staff were especially useful in securing a greater adhesion of the plating to its base. Wright's process turned out to be not quite as perfect as the Elkingtons had hoped when they purchased it from him. Nevertheless, the early troubles were steadily being overcome, and they were confident that it was now only a matter of time before the Sheffield plate trade began to crumble before the sheer weight of the firm's attack.

Before we consider the plight of the Sheffield manufacturers, it is essential to say something of the material with which they worked, and to see how it differed from the new process. Electroplated articles had to be assembled, cleaned and finished before the coating of silver was put on. Many electroplated articles manufactured in the 1840s were in fact cast, either entire or in parts, like the **teapot** illustrated. Sheffield platers found it very hard to adjust to this, because the procedure was virtually the reverse of their own method of manufacture. They worked with a material traditionally said to have been accidentally invented by Thomas Bolsover, a Sheffield cutler, in 1742. The basic principle was that a layer of silver could be fused by means of fire on to one or two sides of a copper ingot, which was then capable of being worked as one metal. The ingot was rolled into sheets, from which the shapes of the articles to be made were stamped out. It was a trade which employed machinery, yet demanded a high

23

degree of skill on the part of the craftsmen who shaped and assembled the components in such a way as to disguise the copper edges of the plate. Casting was used only occasionally; most attached ornamental details were die-stamped.

Antagonistic as they were, the Sheffield platers might have come round sooner to the new process if G. R. Elkington had been less demanding. His initial requirements were that firms to whom he sold a licence to electroplate should make a down payment to the patentees of £1,000, pay a royalty on every ounce of silver deposited, and stamp their wares with Elkington's mark as well as their own. These were stiff terms, and he was very soon to moderate them, reducing his financial demands and withdrawing

Electroplated teapot. Height $5\frac{1}{2}$ in. By James Dixon & Sons, Sheffield. About 1848. Private collection.

Candelabrum-épergne of electroplated nickel silver. Height 29½ in. The centre branches support a glass bowl. By Elkington, Mason & Company. 1855.

the provision about the Elkington mark. But in the meantime he had already made overtures and been rebuffed.

He approached T. J. & N. Creswick in 1841: they hesitated, then turned him down. The same happened with Roberts, Smith & Company. Their refusal was largely prompted by the aged Samuel Roberts senior, an inventor of great distinction in his time. Roberts's last contribution to the Sheffield plating trade in which he had spent his working life was made in 1830, when he took out a patent (no. 5963) covering the interpolation of a layer of nickel alloy between the copper ingot and the silver coating. Nickel, mined in Saxony, was only just beginning to be refined in this country by Percival Norton Johnson of Hatton Garden, London, founder of the firm of Johnson, Matthey & Company. Roberts was one of the first to capitalise on the colour of the nickel: light and cold coloured, it showed the effects of wear far less obviously than copper when the surface plating was rubbed off. Thomas Nicholson, then in partnership in Sheffield with Robert Gainsford, also successfully fused silver to nickel alloy in the same year; after the partnership broke up in 1833, Gainsford continued the practice, as is shown by an entrée dish of 1835. Ironically, after all the pioneering work by the Sheffield platers with nickel alloy, it became the favourite base of the electroplaters.

Old Samuel Roberts was aghast when he learned that serious consideration was being given by the partners of Roberts, Smith & Company to Elkington's proposals. He had nominally retired from business, but this did not prevent him from expressing his opinions forcibly. 'I am persuaded,' he declared, 'that their mode of plating will inevitably be much less used, than you are anticipating', and so the firm held aloof. But other letters exchanged between Samuel Roberts junior and Evan Smith, the London partner, tellingly describe the consequences of their decision. The retailers may have been slow to buy electroplate, but once they did its style and treatment suddenly made Sheffield plate seem old-fashioned, and they no longer wanted it.

The situation deteriorated so rapidly that in May 1843 Smith and Roberts decided to cut their prices by fifty per cent in an effort to dispose of their goods. Samuel Roberts junior wrote despairingly of 'B. Smith's beautiful patterns which have brought things to perfection at once'. His firm at any rate managed to stay in existence, and later, first as Smith, Sissons & Company and then as W. & G. Sissons, they built a new reputation for electroplated and silver wares.

The 'beautiful patterns' cited by Roberts were, of course, the essays in organic naturalism at which Benjamin Smith's artists excelled. Other styles were represented in the pattern books issued by Elkington, Mason & Company during this decade; some of these seem to have come from Smith also. But the naturalistic works predominated, and they were so impressive that despite an intellectual reaction against the style in 1851 Elkington's kept them in production for decades afterwards. The **candelabrum-épergne** illustrated was made in 1855, but it is very close to a pattern dating from 1847 or even earlier.

The Elkingtons were quite extraordinarily fortunate that their sustained drive to launch electroplating coincided with the height of the vogue for naturalistic design, which had its roots, literally and figuratively, in stylistic experiments made during the Regency. The technique of Sheffield plate manufacture, with its construction from sheet metal, did not lend itself to the wholesale imitation of nature demanded by the style; instead of organic representation, it could offer at best naturalistic die-stamped embellishments. The Birmingham firm, seizing their chance, promoted the style through the medium of electrotyping, reproducing nature in metal, vein by vein and hair by hair.

In 1839 an amateur scientist had discovered that a non-metallic substance might be electrotyped if it was first coated with black lead to render it conducting. This opened the way to the electro-

26 typing of real **animals, plants and flowers**. Parkes of Elkington's afterwards perfected another method, using phosphorus as an ingredient, and patented it after a year's trial on 27th June 1843 (no. 9807). The technique evoked a tremendous response from the public. The Prince Consort, who visited Elkington's for the first time in 1844, is said to have had a room set aside in

Buckingham Palace for his electrotyping experiments. Elkington's made kits for sale to would-be scientists; a Mr Palmer of Newgate Street, London, was amongst those who stocked them.

In many ways, the vogue for naturalism accorded well with the current attitude to design in the decorative arts. It was held that the best design consisted of an informed reproduction of historic styles: bad design was simply an ignorant attempt to do the same thing. The naturalistic style may therefore be regarded as a pastiche, not of a man-made manner, but of nature itself, arrived at with all the conscientiousness expected of good design.

It was hardly to be expected that the Elkingtons would develop the one style, however successful it was, at the expense of all the others, and while they were promoting naturalism, they brilliantly exploited another aspect of the antiquarianism of the age, also by means of their electrotypes. In order to do so, they recruited their first designer from the continent, a Danish-born architect named Benjamin Schlick, who had spent most of his working life in Paris. Schlick boasted of high connections and had access

opposite Group of silver electrotypes from nature by Frank Mitchell of Sheffield, 1905, showing that the fashion for coating real objects with silver lasted until the 20th century. City of Sheffield Museum, Weston Park.

below Taper-stick, electrotyped in silver, parcel-gilt. Birmingham hallmark for 1844; maker's mark of Elkington & Company. Length $5\frac{1}{2}$ in. The design, supplied by Schlick, was registered on 24th October 1844. Assay Office Collection, Birmingham.

to collections of antiquities, both public and private, from which he was able to take suitable moulds for the Elkingtons to use. He had a pronounced fondness for classical design, or Renaissance interpretations of the classic.

Schlick never hesitated to improve on the originals if he 27 thought it desirable; his **taper-stick** of 1844 was modelled from a Roman lamp and electrotyped either in silver or in copper with a coating of electro-deposited silver, with or without a stand of his own invention. It is worth noting in passing that while the Elkington firm and their licensees in England tended to use nickel alloy (then known as nickel or German silver, the second name being dropped for patriotic reasons in the 1914–1918 war) as the plating base of their ordinary wares, they invariably employed copper for electrotypes. In France, however, the firm's licensees, Charles Christofle & Company of Paris, who were associated with Elkington's from 1842, preferred copper for their 28 ordinary **electroplated wares** until later in the century.

opposite, left Electroplated tea urn. Lithograph from a catalogue of electroplated wares by Charles Christofle & Cie, Paris. About 1855.

opposite, right Card case. Height $3\frac{3}{4}$ in. Electrotype, silvered and parcel-gilt, from a design by George Stanton. 1852. Inscribed: ELKINGTON MASON & CO. Victoria and Albert Museum, London.

below Group of electrotypes shown by Elkington, Mason & Company at the Great Exhibition of 1851, including the table by Schlick and Stanton. Lithograph from M. Digby Wyatt, *Industrial Arts of the Nineteenth Century,* 1851–1853.

Inkstand of cast nickel alloy and brass, electroplated; red glass bottles. Length 5⅞ in. By Elkington, from a design registered 1st November 1841. Collection of L.B. Chinchen, Esq.

29   Schlick's *tour-de-force* was an **electrotyped table** which was commissioned by the Prince Consort on his second visit to the Newhall Street factory in 1849. It was shown at the Great Exhibition of 1851 and is still to be seen in the State Rooms at Osborne House, built as a seaside retreat on the Isle of Wight by Queen Victoria and the Prince. Schlick provided the mould for the table top from a salver in the Louvre. The supporting stand was designed by George C. Stanton, a young artist who had studied at the local art school. Stanton remained with the firm for some years:

28   an **electrotyped card case** designed by him was shown at the Paris Universal Exhibition of 1855 and again at the International Exhibition held in London in 1862.

    The Elkingtons relied so much on their designs to sell their electroplate that they were genuinely frightened of having them pirated by unscrupulous rivals. Happily, they could seek the protection afforded by the Designs Acts of 1839 and 1842, which gave manufacturers patent rights for patterns for a period of up to three years. Many of Schlick's moulds were protected in this

Plate on the underside of the inkstand (*opposite*), citing the Designs Act of 1839, under which the design was registered.

way, despite the fact that they were largely taken from antique pieces. The Elkington firm made consistent use of the Acts from 1841 onwards. The second design to be registered by G.R. Elkington, an **inkstand** of mainly Rococo and Gothic inspiration, dates from 1st November of that year. The **plate** attached to its base shows the serial system of registration: the design was no. 899.

From 1842 until 1884, a diamond-shaped registry mark was used instead of a serial number (see page 62). In 1884 the classes were abolished and system of serial numbers reintroduced, usually with the prefix 'Rd.' The design registers from 1839 until the early years of this century are now in the possession of the Public Record Office, London.

We have already discussed the effect of the Elkingtons' sustained drive on Roberts, Smith & Company. While they were reduced to near-despair in 1843, Elkington's were negotiating the sale of their first licences to Sheffield firms. Neither of the two manufacturers concerned belonged to the great hierarchy of Sheffield platers. The first, John Harrison, a Britannia metal smith, obtained his licence on 13th June; the second, William Carr Hutton, the son of a Birmingham manufacturer of nickel flatware, on 14th June. The Sheffield platers held out because they were now pinning their hopes on Woolrich refusing to part with his dynamo patent to the Elkingtons. But Woolrich, needing money, sold the rights to Brooke Evans, who was in partnership with Charles Askin as nickel refiners and suppliers, and it was from Brooke Evans that Elkington's acquired the patent in 1846.

This marked the real end of the stand made by the Sheffield

Plate attached to the underside of the coffee-pot (see below).

Coffee pot of electroplated Britannia metal. Height $10\frac{1}{4}$ in. By James Dixon & Sons, Sheffield, from a design registered on 29th January 1850. Private collection.

platers. The Britannia metal smiths had already come over in some numbers. Harrison and Hutton were followed by Walker & Coulson in July 1845 and Broadhead & Atkin the following September. But soon firms with plating interests began to capitulate. James Dixon & Sons, manufacturers of Britannia metal, Sheffield plate and silverwork, had farmed out electroplating work to Walker & Coulson for a while, but decided to apply for a licence in 1848, declaring: 'We have for some time thought it would be to our mutual advantage if we were to take out a licence from you and meet with spirit the electroplating in Sheffield'. They obtained their licence in December, virtually at the same time as H. D. Wilkinson, originally a Britannia metal smith.

Dixon's learned from Elkington, Mason & Company the technique said to have been invented by one of the workmen at Newhall Street, Thomas Fearn, and imparted to Harrison as early as 1846. This was a method of electroplating Britannia metal, a soft variety of pewter compounded of tin, antimony and copper, which was usually shaped into articles by spinning. Steam-powered spinning lathes had been in use in Sheffield since about 1820. The process can best be compared to throwing an earthenware pot on a wheel, although the metal is more difficult to work and has to be levered horizontally against wooden chucks cut to shape. Silver and, eventually, nickel alloy could also be spun as well as stamped; all these metals had to be annealed in the course of working, as indeed they still do.

Smith's naturalistic manner was successfully translated by Dixon's into all the metals in which they worked. They registered a teapot of leaf form on 29th January 1850 and produced a complete service from the design in electroplated Britannia metal, including a **coffee pot**, which was illustrated by the *Journal of Design* later the same year. Dixon's marked the base of the coffee pot with the **registry mark** set in their own frame, together with the word 'electroplated'. They did not use the initials **E. P. B. M.** which soon afterwards came into general use to denote electroplated Britannia metal, just as the letters **E.P.N.S.**, ingeniously spaced so as to imply hallmarks while not directly transgressing the law, indicate that the article concerned was made of electroplated nickel silver. Like the maker's marks, these and other stamps were the cause of much agony and some litigation to the Assay Offices, as we shall see.

Most of the old-established Sheffield platers still found it too painful or too expensive, despite the new reasonableness of G. R. Elkington's demands, to associate themselves openly with the Birmingham firm. Thomas Bradbury & Sons, direct descendants of an 18th-century Sheffield firm, tried out the new process in 1848, but decided against obtaining a licence. But Bradbury's are known to have used the services of J. & C. Ratcliff, who plated for the trade in both Birmingham and Sheffield under licence

above The initials E.P.N.S. for electroplated nickel silver are each stamped in a separate shield.

left The initials E.P.B.M. for electroplated Britannia metal similarly laid out. From an early 20th-century sugar bucket by James Dixon & Sons of Sheffield.

from Elkington's. Their presence saved many other Sheffield concerns from treating directly with the enemy and allowed them to spend a great deal of time in public discussion of John Wright's family and scientific associations with Sheffield, which always seemed to keep their hatred of Elkington's alive.

While they were thus engaged in recrimination, Elkington's were steadily taking out patents all over the world, building up an empire of licensees. Perhaps the Sheffield platers procrastinated too long, for little more than a third of the best-known firms of pre-Victorian days survived into the 1850s. It was a last ironic touch that the die-stamping presses and other technical equipment evolved by the Sheffield platers should have contributed to the greater flexibility of electroplate production at this time.

The situation in Birmingham and London was never as difficult as in Sheffield. Even so, applications for licences probably did not come up to the Elkingtons' expectations until the second half of the 1840s, though London was well ahead. Besides Smith, who was an associate rather than a licensee, Edward Barnard & Sons, manufacturers to the silver trade, plated under licence from 3rd December 1842, and Garrard's, the Crown Jewellers, followed them on 1st May 1843.

Amongst the more interesting Birmingham concerns to acquire a licence in the late 1840s was that of William Gough, silversmith and plater. George Wilkinson, the firm's designer, had studied at the local school of design from 1844 to 1846. One of his works, an interesting pierced salver made by the electro process from a design registered on 16th February 1849, was shown by Gough & Company at the Birmingham exhibition of that year. This exhibition gave manufacturers in the Midland district the welcome chance of a trial run for their wares before the Great Exhibition. Gough's display brought him into prominence; contemporary notices stressed the fact that pierced work, once a favourite form of decoration of the Sheffield platers, was so much easier to achieve when there was no copper core to hide.

Gough went on to show a range of pierced articles at the Great
Exhibition, from which a **salver** and a **butter cooler** were ac-

quired as part of the foundation collection of the new Museum of Manufactures, the ancestor of the Victoria and Albert Museum.

The Elkington firm gave great prominence to both their electrotyped and electroplated wares at the Great Exhibition. Apart from the Schlick/Stanton **table**, there was a specially designed vase celebrating the 'Triumph of Science and Industry', surmounted by the figure of the Prince Consort, and an ambitious gilt and silver **electrotyped casket** set with ceramic portraits of the royal family. The casket was designed by Ludwig Gruner and lent by the Queen. Gruner, a German-born artist, was a favourite of the Prince Consort, who entrusted him with several commissions. The electrotypes made by Elkington's for the royal collec-

right Butter cooler, with a glass liner. Height $5\frac{1}{2}$ in. Electroplated nickel silver. By William Gough & Company, Birmingham. About 1851. Victoria and Albert Museum, London.

left Salver. Diameter $12\frac{1}{2}$ in. Electroplated nickel silver, parcel-gilt. By William Gough & Company, Birmingham. 1849–1851. Victoria and Albert Museum, London.

tions constituted a considerable feather in the firm's cap, and this was recognised by the Jury of the Goldsmithing Section, who awarded the firm a Council Medal, the highest distinction, partly on the grounds of Gruner's casket.

Thus far, it seemed that the Elkingtons had achieved their aim of making electroplating both universal and respectable in the space of little more than ten years. But members of the trade were represented on the Jury, as well as distinguished collectors and artists. We may guess that it was the trade element which was responsible for the Jury's refusal to comment on the merits of electroplating, a refusal worded in such a way as to make it plain that it distrusted and disliked the process. The Jury desired

Casket for jewels. Length 49½ in. Electrotyped, silvered, parcel-gilt and enamelled; set with ceramic portraits of Queen Victoria, the Prince Consort and their children. Designed by Ludwig Gruner, manufactured by Elkington's and lent by the Queen to the 1851 Exhibition. London Museum (royal collections).

'only to commend the artistic application of the discovery', that is, electrotyping, although it was forced to sanction electrogilding because of the health hazard of the old process. The Jury pointedly underlined its disapproval by giving a Prize Medal to Creswick's of Sheffield, one of the two concerns to show Sheffield plate at the exhibition. The other was Padley, Parkin & Staniforth who, like Creswick's, went over unobtrusively to the new process only a few years later, using it amongst other things for a splendid range of **coffee machines** which were one of their specialities.

But there was nothing the Jury could do to prop up the old fused plate industry. A few manufacturers like Creswick's and Dixon's went on producing Sheffield plate as well as electroplate for a while longer, but in diminishing quantities. The victory for Elkington's was complete.

Electroplated coffee machine. Height 14 in. Stamped with the initials and 'hand mark' of Padley, Parkin & Staniforth, who showed only Sheffield plate at the Great Exhibition of 1851. An impressive functional design which must date from about 1855, after they had turned to electroplating.

38

Consolidation and Decline

It was very gratifying for G. R. Elkington when the Jury of the International Exhibition of 1862 ate the words of its predecessor, charmingly attempting to explain away the attitude of the 1851 Jury by pointing out that then, of course, electroplating had been 'a new and untried discovery', which was why the Jurors had spoken 'hesitatingly' of its 'advantages, now so generally admitted.' Sheffield plate was now seen to be dying in public: James Dixon & Sons of Sheffield gained a medal at the 1862 exhibition for the excellence of both their fused and electroplate, but their award was unique. No other firm gained so much as a mention for fused plate. In 1878, the British Commissioners for the Paris Universal Exhibition of that year officially pronounced Sheffield plate dead.

The new-found respectability of electroplate stopped short of the marking systems. Following the practice instituted by Sheffield platers in about 1820, for instance, many electroplaters used the crown as part of their range of marks. This device is the hallmark for silver assayed in Sheffield, and its misuse eventually forced the Guardians of the Sheffield Assay Office to threaten legal action in 1896. Elkington's, who were among the offenders, from this date dropped the crown from their E. & Co. mark. The Birmingham authorities experienced difficulty with some American firms, especially the Gorham Plate Company of Rhode Island, who adopted the anchor, the Birmingham hallmark, as their trade mark in about 1870. Other marks introduced in the second half

This form of the anchor mark, the trade mark of the Gorham Plate Company of Rhode Island since about 1870, appeared on their electroplate from 1905 to 1913.

The trade mark of James Deakin & Sons of Sheffield was a lamp. The firm were never Sheffield platers, and there is consequently no confusion arising from their mark.

of the 19th century did not infringe any active statutes; we may mention here the increasing practice amongst British firms of using a **trade mark** which could be registered from the late 1870s. Nevertheless, even these present their problems, for some of them were old Sheffield platers' marks. The crossed arrows mark used by Creswick's for their Sheffield plate was acquired by W. Hutton & Sons, Elkington's licensees. Henry Wilkinson, also of Sheffield, marked his electroplate from 1852 onwards with the crossed keys symbol he had formerly used on Sheffield plate, and Padley, Parkin & Company did likewise with the hand mark. Hence many pieces of electroplate are thought by their possessors to be old Sheffield plate.

Nevertheless, electroplate was now throughly accepted by the public on all levels of society. As early as January 1849 the *Tablet* had noticed that 'Old families are turning their plate into this new security and some of the noblest names are among the patrons of the patentees'. Fear of burglaries, the desire to re-invest capital otherwise tied up in silverwork, a natural tendency to be attracted by anything new, especially when it also represented Britain's technological prowess, all acted as inducements. By the same token, it was also accepted as suitable for gifts. A handsome **service** of electroplate in the fashionable classical manner was presented to Joseph Chamberlain, the future Liberal statesman who was to represent Birmingham in Parliament for many years, on the occasion of his second marriage in 1868.

Naturally, the techniques of electro-metallurgy were continually being refined and developed. For two decades or more, Elkington's maintained their policy of combining research by their own staff with the acquisition of promising inventions by outsiders, but their purchases were fewer and less comprehensive in character. Some interesting inventions seem to have been passed over for one reason or another. Amongst these was one patented on 24th January 1852 (no. 13,914) by Richard Ford Sturges, a Birmingham manufacturer who had obtained a licence from Elkington's in 1845. Sturges' invention was a method of transferring a prepared pattern formed of wire or a strongly figured substance on to sheets of metal by passing them together

Dessert service. Height of centrepiece 27 in. Electroplated nickel silver, parcel-gilt with glass bowls. Probably designed by A.A. Willms; design registered 11th March 1865; made by Elkington & Company in 1868. Presented to Joseph Chamberlain on his second marriage, 8th June 1868. Part of the civic plate, Birmingham, deposited at the City Museum and Art Gallery.

through rollers. It was an extension of the engraved cylinder system which had been in use for many years, but it was claimed by Sturges and his supporters that his invention could be used to print from leaves and other natural substances. It may well have given a fillip to the vogue for fern, **leaf or flower decoration** that lasted from the 1860s to the 1890s, although much of this was engraved by hand.

Other techniques of decoration include electro-damascening and incrusting, first displayed at the Paris Universal Exhibition of 1867 by Christofle, Elkington's licensee. Elkington's already used less elaborate versions of these processes. Chasing and engraving could also be simulated by etching; engraving alone was imitated by a foot-operated knurling machine, often tooled to produce a **zigzag** effect.

The British trade flourished. Between 1867 and 1878 the export of electroplate, principally to India, the African colonies, Australia and Europe virtually doubled from just over £100,000 annual value to about £200,000. Elkington's trade ranged further and included the United States. Their exports consisted largely of straightforward domestic wares, but electrotypes of historic objects were also in demand. The manufacture of these which Schlick had helped to launch in the 1840s grew into an industry of considerable proportions, sponsored by museums and endorsed by heads of state.

Elkington's had had less success with their equally ambitious plans to use the medium for the execution of original designs. Gruner's casket was one of the most celebrated of these electrotypes to be shown at the Great Exhibition. Others were designed for the firm as a special commission by a French artist, Pierre-Emile Jeannest, who became a permanent employee of Elkington's the following year. During his years with the firm, Jeannest made most of his designs for electrotyping. One of his pieces, a **salt cellar** surmounted by a figure of the Infant Neptune, was electrotyped in pure silver; it may be seen to the right of Schlick's table in whose company it remains at Osborne House. Under Jeannest's direction, other designers working for the firm produced some charming electrotyped pieces like the **pencil box** illustrated.

right Detail from a jug. The zigzag patterning has been produced with the aid of a knurling machine. By James Deakin & Sons, Sheffield. About 1885.

below Christening mug given to a child born in 1869. Height 4¼ in. Electroplated nickel silver, engraved with leaves and grapes. Unmarked. Collection of Miss Alicia Robinson.

below Pencil box. Length 9¼ in. Electrotyped and silvered, with a bas-relief on the lid. By Elkington, Mason & Company. About 1854. Victoria and Albert Museum, London.

Pen tray. Length 10½ in. Electrotyped in copper and silvered. About 1860. Collection of John Culme, Esq.

Nevertheless, after Jeannest's sudden death in 1857, G.R. Elkington bowed to the new fashion for elaborately embossed and chased works made without the aid of any mechanical or electrical contrivance, exemplified by the silver designs of Antoine Vechte, who was employed by the London firm of Hunt & Roskell. Vechte's works were the logical outcome of the contemporary passion for historic styles, for it was proclaimed by many besides Pugin that it was useless and dishonest to revive the styles without returning to the old methods of craftsmanship which matched them.

Hunt & Roskell enjoyed a tremendous success at the 1851 exhibition with their display of Vechte's work. Even the Prince Consort, dedicated as he was to the promotion of British technology, was completely overwhelmed by his craftsmanship. Elkington's, who always aspired to keep abreast if not ahead of fashion, were unable to recruit Vechte, so in 1859 they brought over from Paris his pupil, Léonard Morel-Ladeuil, together with an experienced designer of silverwork, A. A. Willms, who became head of their design studio. Willms seems to have made a few designs directly for electrotyping. Even Morel-Ladeuil, *par excellence* the artist-craftsmen, probably did likewise: the **pen tray** illustrated has a cherub and strapwork that can be paralleled in his silver. The trouble is that his designs may have been interpreted and slightly sentimentalised for mass-produced electrotypes by his fellow-countryman, Willms, who was almost certain-

44

ly responsible for the **fruit dish** registered under the Designs
Acts on 16th March 1871. Most of the great set pieces of Morel-
Ladeuil, astonishingly complex exercises in virtuoso craftsmanship like the 'Milton Shield' of 1867 (now in the Victoria and
Albert Museum) which occupied him for months if not years at a
time, were electrotyped by Elkington's, who recouped the
expense of the originals by selling copies on a large scale.

Elkington's had early proof that this policy was rewarding. A
shield embellished with the Battle of the Amazons, made by
Vechte and acquired by the King of Prussia, was reproduced in
electrotype by the firm, who showed one of their copies at the

left Fruit dish with swing handle.
Diameter 8 in. Electroplated; the base
plate possibly electrotyped. Design
registered 16th March 1871.

right Electrotype of Vechte's Amazon
shield for the King of Prussia. One of
these copies was shown by Elkington's
at the 1851 exhibition.
Chromolithograph from M. Digby
Wyatt, *Industrial Arts of the
Nineteenth Century*, 1851–1853.

1851 exhibition. With Gruner's casket, the electrotyped shield was seized on with evident relief by the Jury, whose driving motive was to avoid endorsing electroplate, as we have seen, and cited in the award of a Council Medal to Elkington's: 'These works of art and ornament offer the best specimens of the application of the electrotype process for the exact reproduction of objects in copper, and of precious metals to ornamental purposes'.

Four electrotypes of the Vechte shield were acquired for the new Museum of Manufactures in 1852. The museum became known in 1857 as the South Kensington museum before finally (as far as its art collections were concerned) becoming the Victoria and Albert Museum. The man who became in effect the first Director of the Museum was Henry (later Sir Henry) Cole, who in 1852 was given the complex task of running it while at the same time directing all the state-aided art schools throughout the country. From 1853 his organisation was styled the Science and Art Department. The reasoning behind Cole's appointment was simple. He had the trust of the Prince Consort, who took his self-imposed duties as leader of the country's cultural establishment very seriously, and he was one of the few people who could claim to be something of an authority on design and manufactures. Cole had done brilliantly as a member of the Executive Committee of the Great Exhibition. Now his task was to train designers for industry, to provide good examples of contemporary and historic work for them to study and to try and improve the standard of public taste. The museum was essential to all three functions, objects being circulated round the provinces as part of the educational programme.

Cole and most of his associates had themselves been attracted by the naturalistic style in the 1840s, when he and his friends designed for the decorative arts under the title of '**Felix Summerly's Art Manufactures**'. But the sight of so much unbridled imitation of nature in the British Courts at the Great Exhibition revolted them, and they turned to the safety and discipline of the classic styles. Cole soon saw the potential of electrotypes as a teaching tool, and on 6th October 1853 the Science and Art Department concluded an agreement with Elkington's, by which

47

the latter were granted the right of making reproductions of works belonging to or lent to the museum. These electrotypes bore the **official stamp** of the Department and were sold both by the museum and by Elkington's. Other reproductions made by the firm without the authority of the Department bore the firm's own mark of a horizontal diamond enclosing the usual Elkington & Co. under a crown.

left The oval stamp applied to electrotypes officially approved by the Science and Art Department under the agreement with Elkington's of 6th October 1853.

below A set of decanter stoppers designed for Summerly's Art Manufactures by J.C. Horsley and produced in both silver and electroplate by Benjamin Smith, Elkington's associate. Woodcut illustration from the Summerly catalogue.

There was invariably a strong bias towards **classically derived design** in the selection of objects for electrotyping. Cole became increasingly enthusiastic about the scheme and negotiated with museums and collectors on the continent for permission to copy their objects. His exertions were crowned with a display of electrotypes and plaster casts from South Kensington at the Paris 1867 exhibition, which led to the 'Convention for promoting universal Reproduction of Works of Art for the benefit of Museums of all Countries'. The signatories were 'several princes of the reigning families of Europe', including the Prince of Wales, later King Edward VII, and the Cesarevitch Nicholas of Russia.

below Electrotyped copy of an English goblet of 1616 in a Moscow Treasury; one of the reproductions made by Elkington's on their official visit to Russia in 1880–1881. Height 18 in. Victoria and Albert Museum, London.

left Electrotyped ewer, silvered and parcel-gilt. Height 11¼ in. After a well known piece by the French Renaissance artist, François Briot (about 1550–about 1616). Victoria and Albert Museum, London.

The Convention played a considerable part in opening up collections of metalwork in areas unknown even to scholars, as in the case of Russia. It was 1880 before Cole's successor at South Kensington was informed by Wilfrid Cripps, an authority on silver, that he had been told of a 'Treasury full at Moscow:–much of it said to be old and massive English plate [used in the sense of objects made of gold or silver] imported by Peter the Great'. As a result of this surprising information, a young representative of the Department was despatched to Russia later in the year, accompanied by a team of moulders and casters from Elkington's. The tragi-comic story of their sojourn in Russia deserves to be related at greater length than is possible here. We can only note in passing their difficulties with climate and language. They were also pursued by irate owners angered by the appearance of their treasures after the craftsmen had made moulds from them, although it was claimed that much of the seeming damage was caused by 'soap or oil remaining which has been used for the process, and which in a short time will disappear'. The fuss died down, cordial relations were resumed and some magnificent reproductions of **English silverwork** from the 16th to the 18th centuries were amongst the great haul brought back by the expedition.

48

Electrotypes formed part of the first collections of several museums, including the Metropolitan Museum of New York, whose foundation owed something to the example of South Kensington. After dealing with such momentous international forays it is perhaps something of an anticlimax to return to the subject of electroplate, although in its new classical manifestation it was often very handsome. The newest fashion was the so-called Etruscan style, based on the forms and decoration of Graeco-Roman antiquities. It represented the antithesis of naturalism: it was symmetrical, formal and controlled; its decoration, whether or not engraved as in the **coffee pot** illustrated, was always subservient to the form of the article. In the course of time, as eclecticism rather than strict antiquarianism became the ideal, the style lent itself to some striking variations on the classic theme, exemplified by a **pedestal table** of 1862 now in the Boston Museum of Fine Arts, perhaps adapted from a centrepiece.

50

50

left Electroplated coffee pot from a tea and coffee service. Height 10¾ in. The classic shape is surmounted by an Assyrian lion, inspired by the publication of Layard's finds at Nineveh. Probably by a Sheffield firm. About 1860. Private collection.

below left Electroplated coffee pot. Height 11 in. By Roberts & Belk, Sheffield. About 1867. Collection of Messrs Roberts & Belk.

below Electroplated pedestal table, the base probably designed by A.A. Willms and registered in November 1862. Height 29 in. The Museum of Fine Arts, Boston, Massachusetts (Theodora Wilbour Fund in memory of Charlotte Beebe Wilbour).

Electroplated tray. Length 16 in. The swage or rim executed from a model by Alfred Stevens. By Thomas Bradbury & Sons, Sheffield. 1856. Victoria and Albert Museum, London.

Elkington's, the makers, registered a series of these designs on 22nd and 26th November. Of the acceptable alternatives to the classical manner, the Assyrian style was perhaps the most interesting. Layard's publication of his findings at Nineveh prompted a few essays in the manner at about the time of the Great Exhibition, but it was a decade before it caught on to any extent. The **coffee pot** illustrated is a charming example of commercial Assyrian.

The Etruscan style continued to be fashionable throughout the 1850s to the 1870s, shading off into the Robert Adam or Louis XVI revival, which resulted in some pleasant imitations of late 18th-century shapes and a rather freer rendering of the characteristic 'bright-cut' engraving, so-called because the craftsman worked with short flicks of his tool to catch the light.

As the 1850s progressed, the soft contours and slow transitions from angle to angle which marked most design in whatever manner began increasingly to give way to a more pronounced outline, sharp uprights contrasting with emphatic horizontals. One of the designers who helped to launch this treatment was the sculptor Alfred Stevens, an exponent of the High Renaissance manner and a favourite of Henry Cole and his circle. Stevens began designing for the metalworking trades in Sheffield just before the Great Exhibition, when he was living in the town. Though he returned to London shortly afterwards, he continued to send models for silver and electroplate to Thomas Bradbury & Sons. He provided the models for the **plated tray** illustrated here. During the years

51

he spent in Sheffield, Stevens gathered around him a group of acolytes from the local art school; the best known, who came to work for Cole at South Kensington, was Godfrey Sykes, who adhered closely to the master's style but, as in his **tobacco jar**, invested it with more gentleness.

The influence of South Kensington began to wane towards the end of the 1860s. Henry Cole, who had hitherto made his presence felt in the manufacturing world through both his educational activities and his continuing connection with international exhibitions, retired in 1873. His phenomenal energy had made it possible for him to have many irons in the fire simultaneously, but towards the end of his career he was defeated by forces outside himself. The rise of the medieval movement, of which Pugin had been the first prophet, had meant that Cole lost to its ranks a younger generation of designers and theorists who might otherwise have come to renew the now stultifying ideology of South Kensington. Ruskin had become the arch-apostle of the medievalists, and it so happened that he detested the methods used by the South Kensington circle to train its students almost as much as he disliked the mechanised trades for which they were intended. He said so, and his views were damaging to Cole.

52

The silver and plating trade itself was beginning to show signs of flagging inspiration in its upper reaches. In an attempt to expand production, manufacturers turned out steadily increasing quantities of 'novelties', many of them in electroplate. They were simply following the precedent of the 18th-century Sheffield platers, who had found it profitable to make items such as egg frames, coffee machines and many similar accoutrements for the table. **Egg frames** were still popular, as were traditional wares like **dish covers** and kettles on stands which were in fact far from being novelties, but were part of the serious business of eating and drinking. It was the self-appointed task of manufacturers, then as now, to convince the public that it could scarcely conduct its everyday domestic affairs without a great variety of ancillary items. **Crumb scoops**, breakfast frames, luncheon frames, pickle frames, conserve stands, hors d'œuvres dishes, spoon warmers, sardine boxes, biscuit boxes, syphons and champagne holders were amongst the pieces urged upon purchasers. It may be suspected that a great many of these were designed especially as wedding presents.

In the 'Aesthetic' 1870s the doctrines of the medievalists gained increasing acceptance, although it was the Japanese manner which provided the newest and most popular visual stimulus. The trade fought hard to keep up with the times. The electro-processes scarcely lent themselves to reproducing the subtleties of Japanese craftsmanship, but at least they could encompass the popular features of design. Segmented asymmetrical decoration, fans, **cranes, foliage**, badges and vaguely oriental buildings were all grist to the mill.

It was rarer for manufacturers to reproduce the actual forms of Japanese articles. Ironically, the one designer working for the metal trades who brilliantly absorbed the essentials of Japanese work and recreated them in a manner acceptable to Western tastes was a product of South Kensington. Dr Christopher Dresser

Two electroplated crumb scoops. *Above*: length 12½ in. By Mappin & Webb. About 1890. Collection of Mrs Barbara Morris. *Below*: length 13¾ in. Ivory handle. Unmarked. About 1880. Private collection.

opposite Electroplated tea and coffee service, from a catalogue issued by Silber & Fleming, suppliers to the trade, 1889. The form of the articles is early 19th-century, though the handles are inspired by Dresser. The decoration is Japanese.

(his Ph.D. was an honorary degree from the University of Jena) had been a student at the London school in the 1840s and remained under the Cole regime to become a lecturer in botany there. He afterwards became a freelance designer in several media, a writer, lecturer and an enthusiastic but, it appears, somewhat unsuccessful businessman. Having been appointed art adviser to a London firm importing Japanese goods, Dresser visited Japan in 1876 in a quasi-official capacity, buying for his employers, the South Kensington authorities and for Tiffany's of New York. His designs for silver and electroplate made after this visit were purchased by Elkington's, Hukin & Heath's of Birmingham, by Dixon's of Sheffield and probably by other firms also.

57   The handles of his **teapots** and claret jugs were directly inspired by those of the Japanese pieces that he imported, but other features of his designs stem from his concern for functionalism, which may be attributed to his connection with South Kensington. He always bore the machine in mind when he made his designs: hence, unlike Japanese work, the surface of his metalwork was invariably unornamented.

Dresser's designs were plagiarised by the trade. Versions of his 57   **decanters** and his wire toast and letter racks were manufactured by such firms as Mappin & Webb and James Deakin & Sons, both of Sheffield. Their clean, stark lines, in astonishing contrast to the heavily worked Renaissance, Neo-classical, Rococo and Gothic designs to be seen in pattern books and trade catalogues of the time, struck a responsive chord in the hearts of the devotees of Aestheticism, and all the copies of his work seem to have sold well. They were virtually the only designs to break the perpetual cycle of revivals: the Rococo style, for instance, was enjoying its second round of popularity in the century.

The realisation that manufacturers in general could no longer be regarded as providing an original force in the creation of fashion gave added strength to a group of rebels inspired by Ruskin and William Morris. They were determined to make a final break with industry and its unthinking historicism. The outcome was the Arts and Crafts movement of the 1880s.

Most of the Arts and Crafts designers were their own execu-

above Electroplated teapot with ebony handle. Height 5½ in. Stamped with the name of the designer: 'Chr. Dresser'. Made by James Dixon & Sons, Sheffield. 1879. Collection of Messrs James Dixon & Sons.

left Decanter. Height 9½ in. Glass, mounted in electroplate, with wooden handle. Made by James Deakin & Sons of Sheffield in imitation of a design by Christopher Dresser. About 1885. Private collection.

tants, or they worked in conjunction with a small group of crafts-men who could be relied upon to carry out their designs sympathetically. W. A. S. Benson, an established member of the Morris circle, differed from the rest in that he designed specifically for machine production and had his own factory at Hammersmith. His works were usually executed in copper and brass, or in **electroplate**. Their excellence was appreciated by S. Bing, the founder of the Parisian shop, L'Art Nouveau. He stocked Benson's wares and also used them in his display at the Paris 1900 exhibition.

Other more conventional Arts and Crafts metalworkers like Alexander Fisher and Nelson Dawson also made use of electroplate, which was not regarded as the prerogative of the trade. C. R. Ashbee employed it on occasion for some of the **stock pieces** made by his Guild of Handicraft.

C. R. Ashbee, like most of his friends, was an articulate observer and critic of the trade, occasionally inclined to overemphasis but interesting nonetheless. He visited the United States in 1896 and again in 1901 in order to recruit support for the National Trust. On both occasions he took the opportunity of visiting factories and workshops, and his comments on the Gorham Manufacturing Company at Providence, Rhode Island, on the occasion of his second visit are worth recording, for they throw light not only on the American situation but on the English trade as well.

Ashbee noted 'that the application of machinery has been carried to a pitch of excellence and precise skill in its use for the making of silver ware [and presumably electroplated articles as well] which no firm in England can come anywhere near.' This compliment was modified by his remark that 'really individual work', that is, the kind of articles produced by his Guild, had no parallel in America. But 'in England', he said, 'the great Silversmiths' houses are dying, they have not the capital nor the means nor the wits to put in the newest American machinery, nor the brains, even if it were possible to do so, to accept and work in with the Arts and Crafts movement'. Codman, the Company's chief designer and himself an Englishman, told Ashbee that their 'skilled labour comes largely from England . . . 7 out of 10 are

Electroplated coffee pot and cream jug. Height of coffee pot $7\frac{3}{4}$ in. Designed by W.A.S. Benson and made at his Hammersmith (London) factory. About 1905. Victoria and Albert Museum, London.

Englishmen from the great houses, Mappins...Elkingtons' and others. Codman said of Elkington's: 'the whole thing's dead!'

It was to be expected that Ashbee, as an upholder of Arts and Crafts ideals, would disapprove of the Gorham Company's designs, much as he admired their machinery. But the remarks quoted above underline the fact that since Tiffany's had swept the board with their Japanese-inspired work at the Paris Exhibition of 1878, the initiative had passed from England to the United States. In early Victorian times, English silversmiths had been able to lure French craftsmen over to help build up their own businesses, but now silversmiths and designers in search of better conditions were able to go to America, abandoning their English employers.

But sadly, in the end it was Ashbee's Guild that perished, forced into dissolution by commercial firms who had suddenly realised that they could plagiarise Arts and Crafts originality as well as historic styles.

Resurgence

Electroplating has continued in the 20th century, although as a medium for advanced design it lost ground to chromium plate in the 1920s and 1930s, and to stainless steel after the second World War.

With the disappearance of historicism as the basis of design, which was the most enduring contribution of the Arts and Crafts movement, there seemed to be no grounds for the continuance of electrotyping except for the most specialised purposes. But very recently there has been a new patent for electrotyping, an improvement on the old techniques, which has given the process a new life and impetus.

61   The **coronet** here illustrated is already celebrated all over the world: designed by Louis Osman, it was worn by the Prince of Wales at his Investiture at Caernarvon Castle on 1st July 1969.

left Electroplated muffin dish, set with a chrysoprase. Designed by C.R. Ashbee and made by the Guild of Handicraft. About 1900. Height $4\frac{1}{2}$ in. Victoria and Albert Museum, London.

The Prince of Wales's coronet. From a design and model by Louis Osman. Electrotyped in gold and set with emeralds and diamonds by B.J.S. Electroplating Limited and Engelhard Industries Limited. Engraved by Malcolm Appleby. 1969. Royal collections.

Marks

The earliest electroplate made by Elkington's was marked with 'E & Co' crowned in a shield and the word ELEC TRO PLATE in three portions.

1840

1841

In 1841 and again in 1842 the mark was changed and a date number was added.

1842–1864

1865–1897

1849–1864

This series of numbers ran from 1 to 8 (the 6 was reversed: ∂) until 1849 when the series was altered to letters, beginning with K. With the beginning of the new series of letters in 1865 the mark was also changed. The date letters missed out B, C, I and J, while Q, not used by the sheet department and only partially by the cast department, was used as well as R in 1877. Slightly different marks were used in 1898–1899 and from 1900 onwards.

1865–1885

1886–1911

1912–1936